THE LIBRARY
POP SONGS

AMSCO PUBLICATIONS
PART OF THE MUSIC SALES GROUP
LONDON/NEW YORK/PARIS/SYDNEY/COPENHAGEN/BERLIN/MADRID/HONG KONG/TOKYO

MUSIC COMPILED AND PROCESSED BY CAMDEN MUSIC SERVICES.

THIS BOOK COPYRIGHT © 2015 BY AMSCO PUBLICATIONS,
A DIVISION OF MUSIC SALES CORPORATION, NEW YORK

ORDER NO. AM1006104

EXCLUSIVE DISTRIBUTORS:
MUSIC SALES LIMITED
14–15 BERNERS STREET, LONDON W1T 3LJ, UK.
MUSIC SALES CORPORATION
180 MADISON AVENUE, 24TH FLOOR, NEW YORK NY 10016, USA.
MUSIC SALES PTY. LIMITED
UNITS 3-4, 17 WILLFOX STREET, CONDELL PARK NSW 2200, AUSTRALIA.

PRINTED CHINA.

Contents

Always On My Mind

Elvis Presley

Words & Music by Mark James,
Wayne Thompson & Johnny Christopher

Bleeding Love

Leona Lewis

Words & Music by Ryan Tedder & Jesse McCartney

Babylon

David Gray

Words & Music by David Gray

1. Fri - day night__ and I'm go - in' no - where, all the lights__ are chan - gin' green__
(Verse 2 see block lyric)

Verse 2:
Saturday an' I'm runnin' wild
An' all the lights are changin' red to green
Movin' through the crowds, I'm pushin'
Chemicals are rushin' in my bloodstream
Only wish that you were here
You know I'm seein' it so clear
I've been afraid to show you how I really feel
Admit to some o' those bad mistakes I've made.

Well, if you want it come an' get it *etc.*

Bridge Over Troubled Water

Simon & Garfunkel

Words & Music by Paul Simon

Moderate, not too fast, like a spiritual

rubato

1. When you're

wea - ry,___ feel - in___ small,

(2.) down and out,___ when you're on the street,

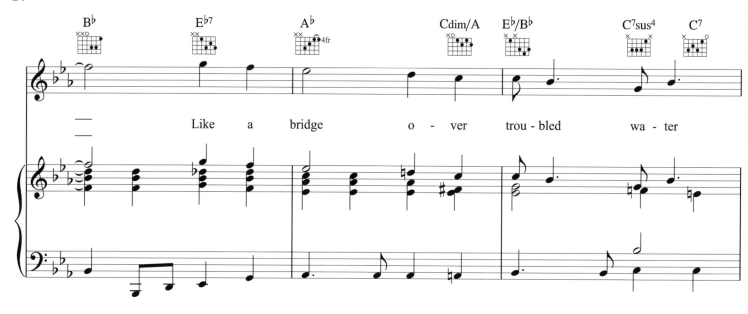

Like a bridge o - ver trou - bled wa - ter

I will lay me down. Like a bridge o - ver

trou-bled wa-ter I will lay me down.

rubato

2. When you're

2.

trou-bled wa-ter I will lay me down.

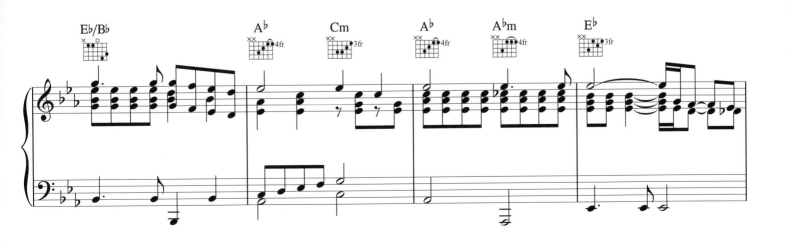

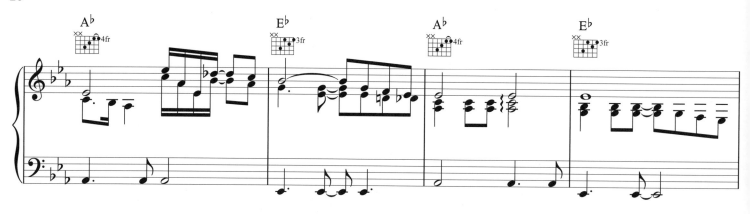

Sail on sil-ver girl, sail on by.

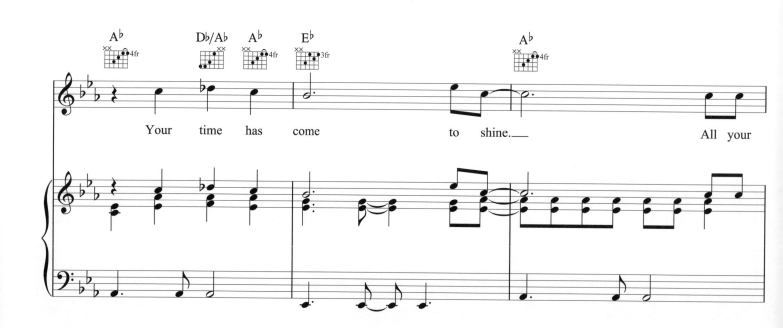

Your time has come to shine.___ All your

Candle In The Wind

Elton John

Words & Music by Elton John & Bernie Taupin

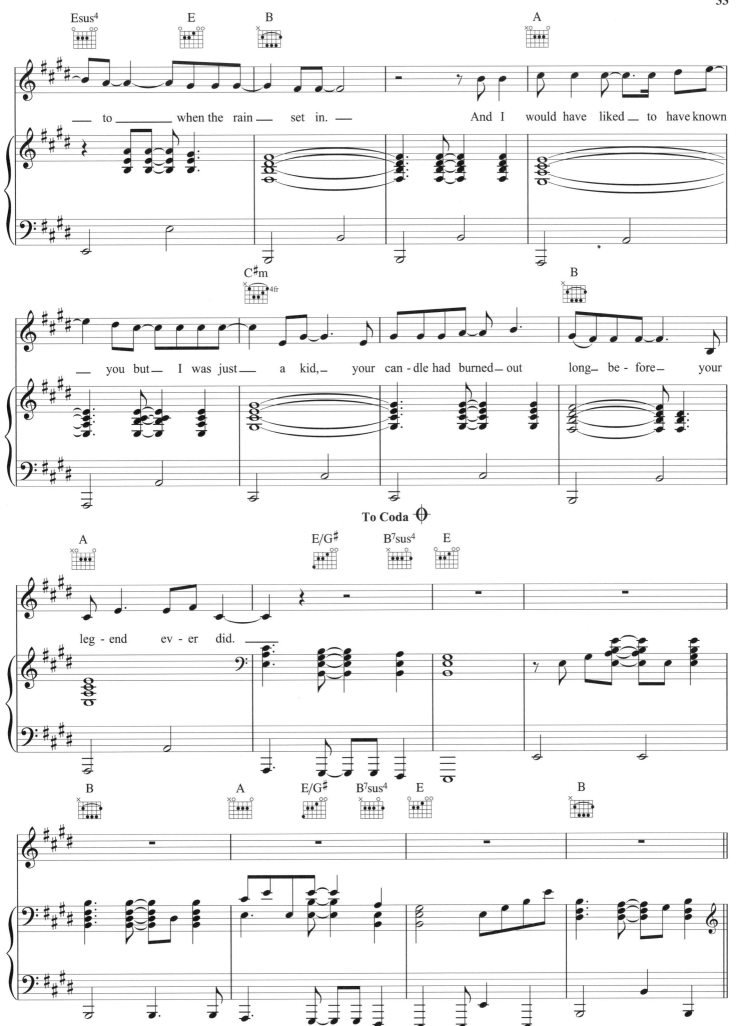

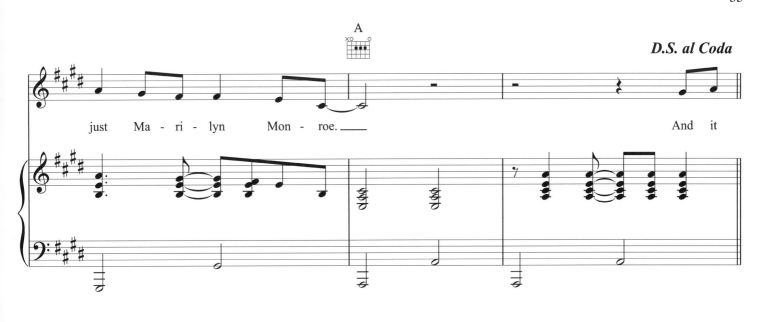

D.S. al Coda

just Ma - ri - lyn Mon - roe._____ And it

⊕ Coda

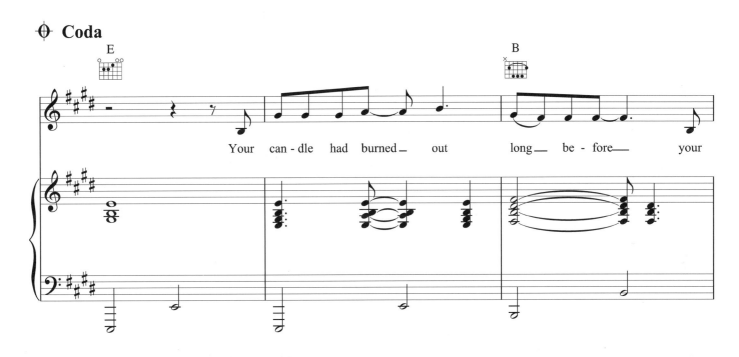

Your can - dle had burned___ out long___ be - fore___ your

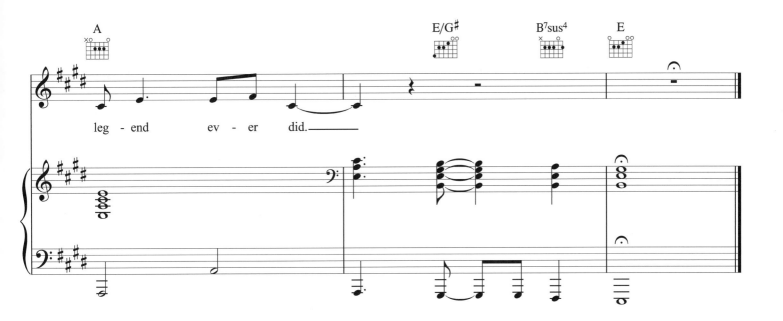

leg - end ev - er did._____

Clocks

Coldplay

Words & Music by Guy Berryman, Chris Martin,
Jon Buckland & Will Champion

1. The lights go out and I can't be saved, tides that I tried to
2. Con-fu-sion that never stops, the clos-ing walls and the

And noth - ing else com - pares.___

And noth - ing else com - pares.___

1 & 2° *Tacet* You_____ are.___

Home, home,___ where I want to go.

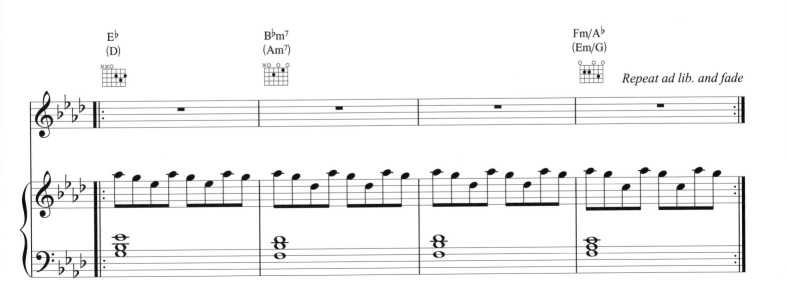

(They Long To Be) Close To You

The Carpenters

Words by Hal David
Music by Burt Bacharach

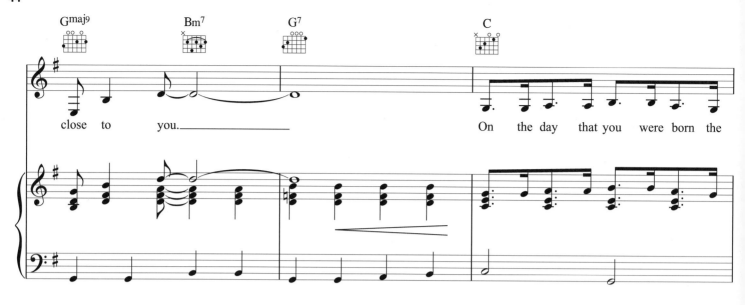

close to you._____ On the day that you were born the

an - gels got to - ge - ther___ And de - ci - ded to cre - ate a dream come

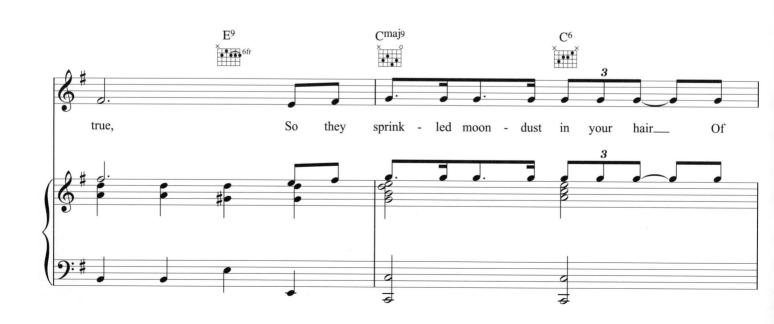

true, So they sprink - led moon - dust in your hair___ Of

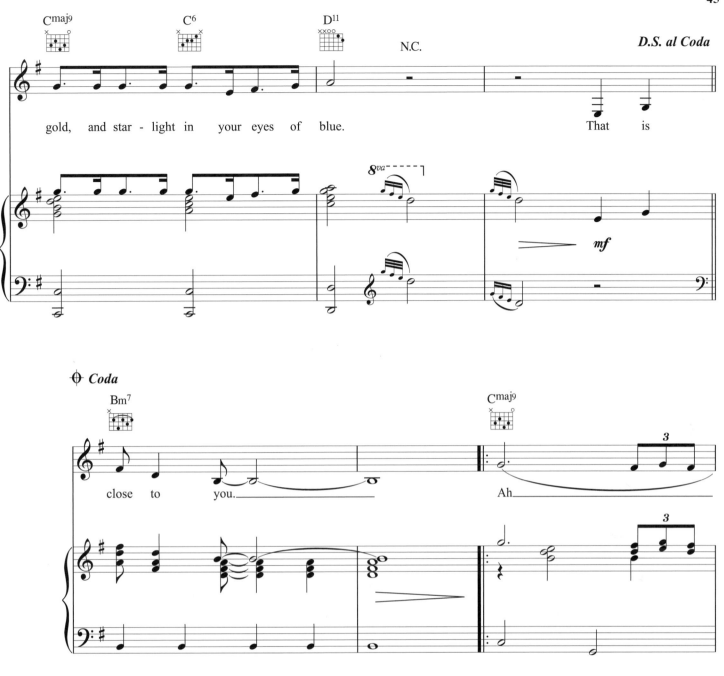

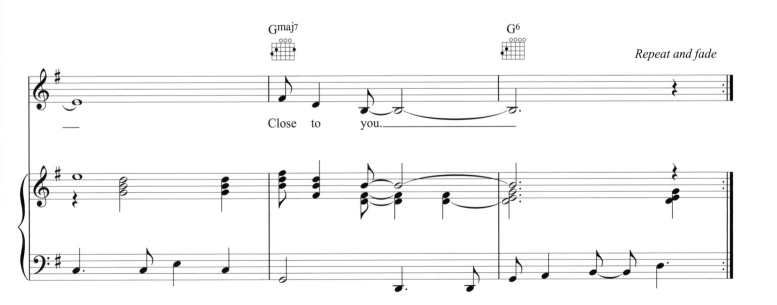

Crazy

Gnarls Barkley

Words & Music by Thomas Callaway, Brian Burton,
Gianfranco Reverberi & Gian Piero Reverberi

Dancing Queen

ABBA

Words & Music by Benny Andersson,
Stig Anderson & Björn Ulvaeus

Don't Know Why

Norah Jones

Words & Music by Jesse Harris

To Coda ⊕

Gm7 C7 F7sus4 B♭ B♭7 Gm7 C7

I don't know why___ I did - n't come,___ I don't know why_ I did - n't_

F7sus4 B♭ B♭maj7 B♭7 E♭maj7 D7

__ come._ 2. When I saw_____ the break__ of day_

(Verse 3 see block lyric)

Gm7 C7 F7sus4 B♭ F11 B♭maj7 B♭7

I wished that I_____ could fly___ a - way,_ 'stead of kneel - ing in

E♭maj7 D7 Gm7 C7 F7sus4 B♭

the sand, catch - ing tear - drops in my___ hand._ My

Verse 3:
Out across the endless sea
I will die in ecstasy
But I'll be a bag of bones
Driving down the road alone.

My heart is drenched in wine etc.

Verse 4:
Something has to make you run
I don't know why I didn't come
I feel as empty as a drum
I don't know why I didn't come
I don't know why I didn't come
I don't know why I didn't come

Don't Stop Believin'

Journey

Words & Music by Steve Perry,
Neal Schon & Jonathan Cain

1. Just a   small town   girl,___   liv - ing   in   a
3. Walk - ing hard to   get   my   fill.___   Ev -'ry - bod - y

2. A sing-er in a smo-key room,— the smell of wine— and cheap per-fume.—

For a smile— they can share the night. It goes on and on— and on— and on.—

Don't_ stop be - liev - in'. Hold on to that feel - ing._____

Repeat ad lib. to fade

Street - light peo - ple. Oh._____

Eternal Flame

The Bangles

Words & Music by Susanna Hoffs,
Tom Kelly & Billy Steinberg

Say my name,— sun shines through the rain,———— a whole

life so lone - ly——— and then come and ease— the pain.———

I don't wan - na lose this feel - ing.

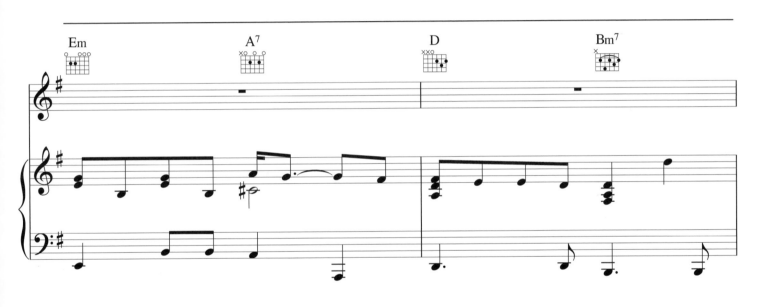

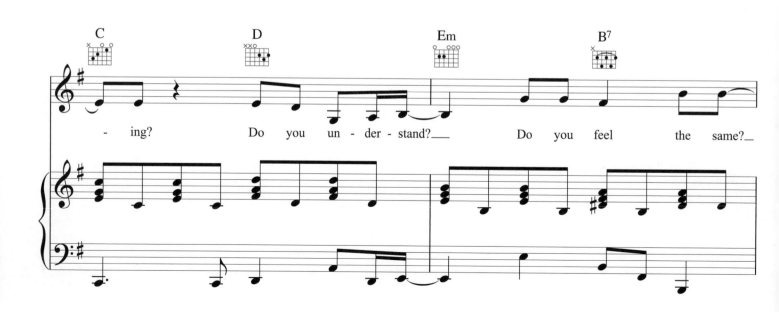

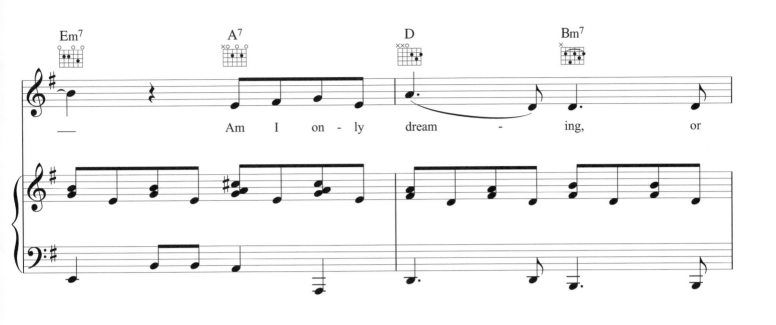

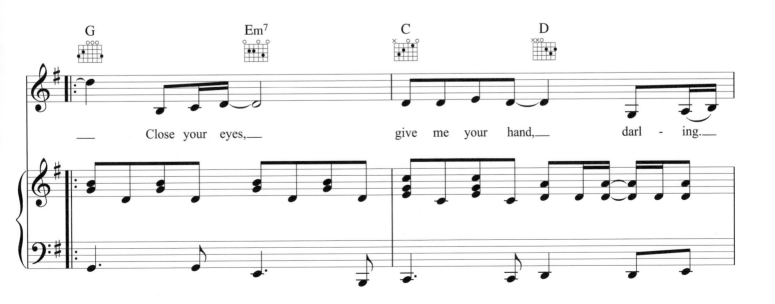

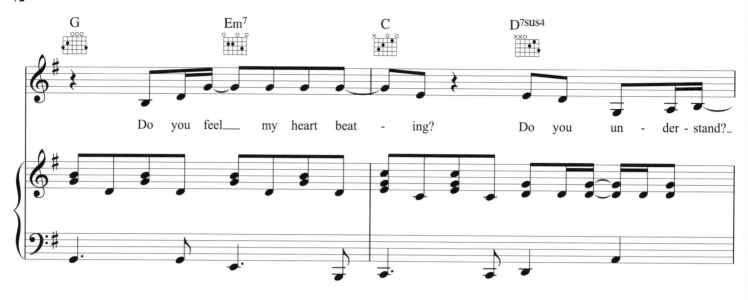

Do you feel___ my heart beat - ing? Do you un - der - stand?___

___ Do you feel the same?___ Am I on - ly

Repeat to fade

dream - ing, is this burn - ing an e - ter - nal flame?___

Every Breath You Take

The Police

Words & Music by Sting

Eye Of The Tiger

Survivor

Words & Music by Jim Peterik & Frank Sullivan III

Family Affair

Mary J. Blige

Words & Music by Mary J. Blige, Bruce Miller,
Andre Young, Melvin Bradford, Mike Elizondo,
Camara Kambon, Asiah Louis & Luchana Lodge

Verse 2:
It's only gonna be about a matter of time
Before you get loose and start to lose your mind
Cop you a drink, go 'head and rock your ice
'Cause we celebrating No More Drama in our life
With a great track pumpin', everybody's jumpin'
Go ahead and twist your back and get your body bumpin'
I told you leave your situations at the door
So grab somebody and get your ass on the dance floor.

Let's get it crunk, we gon' have fun up on it *etc.*

From A Distance

Bette Midler

Words & Music by Julie Gold

Fireflies

Owl City

Words & Music by Adam Young

$\quad$ = 96

N.C.

N.C.

1. You would not be-lieve your eyes   if ten___ mil-lion fire-flies
2. 'Cause I'd___ get a thou-sand hugs   from ten___ thou-sand light-ning bugs

Grenade

Bruno Mars

Words & Music by Philip Lawrence, Peter Hernandez,
Christopher Brown, Ari Levine, Claude Kelly & Andrew Wyatt

Hallelujah

Leonard Cohen

Words & Music by Leonard Cohen

How Deep Is Your Love

The Bee Gees

Words & Music by Barry Gibb, Maurice Gibb & Robin Gibb

I know your eyes in the morn - ing sun.___
I be - lieve in you.___
I feel you touch___ me in the pour - ing rain___
You know the door___ to my ver - y

And the mo - ment that you wan - der far___ from me,___ I wan - na
You're the light___ in my deep - est, dark - est hour;___ you're my

Have I Told You Lately

Van Morrison

Words & Music by Van Morrison

do.

There's a love that's di - vine___

and it's yours and it's mine,___ like the sun.___

At the end of the day___

we should give thanks and pray to the One.

3, 5. Have I

Hey Jude

The Beatles

Words & Music by John Lennon & Paul McCartney

Hey, Soul Sister

Train

Words & Music by Espen Lind, Pat Monahan & Amund Bjorklund

Honey Honey

ABBA

Words & Music by Benny Andersson,
Stig Anderson & Björn Ulvaeus

Ho - ney, ho - ney, how__ you thrill__ me, a - ha, ho - ney, ho - ney.
Ho - ney, ho - ney, let__ me feel__ it, a - ha, ho - ney, ho - ney.
Ho - ney, ho - ney, touch__ me ba - by, a - ha, ho - ney, ho - ney.

Ho - ney, ho - ney, near - ly kill__ me, a - ha, ho - ney, ho - ney.
Ho - ney, ho - ney, don't__ con - ceal__ it, a - ha, ho - ney, ho - ney.
Ho - ney, ho - ney, hold__ me ba - by, a - ha, ho - ney, ho - ney.

I'd
The
You

heard a-bout you___ be - fore,_____ I want-ed to know___ some more,_____ And
way that you kiss___ good - night,_____ the way that you hold___ me tight,_____ I
look like a mo - vie star,_____ but I know just how___ you are,_____ And

now I know what___ they mean,_____ you're a love ma - chine._____ Oh, you make me diz - zy.
feel like I wan - na sing,_____ when you do your thing,___ yeah.
ho - ney, to say___ the least,_____ you're a dog - gone beast,___ yeah.

I don't wan - na hurt___ you ba - by, I

Human Nature

Michael Jackson

Words & Music by Steve Porcaro & John Bettis

1. Look-ing   out____   'cross____ the night-time,   the cit-y winks a sleep-less

(funky 'off-beat' feel throughout)

(Everything I Do) I Do It For You

Bryan Adams

Written by Michael Kamen, Bryan Adams & Robert John Lange

1.Look in-to my eyes,_____ you will see_____

(vers 2 see bloack lyric)

what you mean to_____ me. Search your heart,_____ search your

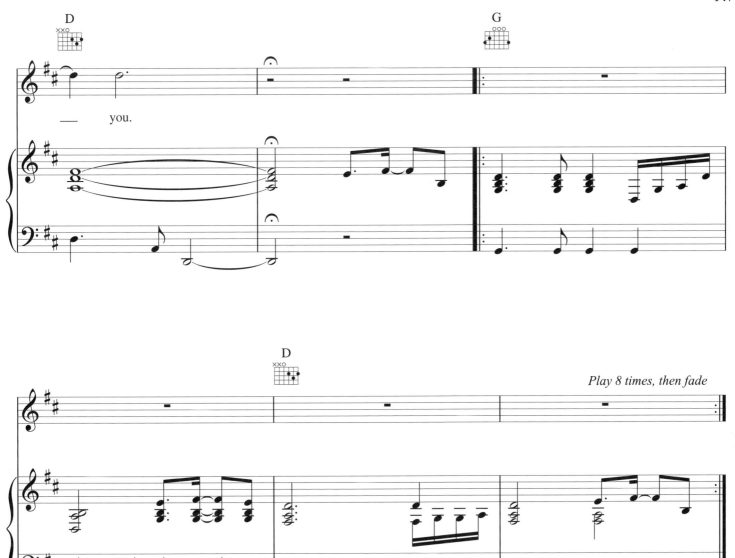

Verse 2:
Look into your heart, you will find
There's nothin' there to hide.
Take me as I am, take my life
I would give it all, I would sacrifice
Don't tell me it's not worth fightin' for
I can't help it, there's nothin' I want more.
You know it's true, everything I do
I do it for you.

I Will Always Love You

Whitney Houston

Words & Music by Dolly Parton

I Will Survive

Gloria Gaynor

Words & Music by Dino Fekaris & Freddie Perren

If You Leave Me Now

Chicago

Words & Music by Peter Cetera

Original key: B major

♩ = 100

Lyrics:

If you leave me now___ you'll take a-way the big-gest part___ of me, ooh,___ no,___ ba-by, please___ don't go.___

things we said___ to - day._____ If you

leave me now___ you'll take a - way the big - gest part___ of me,___

no,___ ba-by, please___ don't go.___

Ooh,___ ma-ma, I've just got to have___ your lov - ing, yeah.___

Repeat and fade

It Must Be Love

Madness

Words & Music by Labi Siffre

It must be love,___ love, love

Isn't She Lovely

Stevie Wonder

Words & Music by Stevie Wonder

Just Dance

Lady Gaga

Words & Music by Aliaune Thiam,
Stefani Germanotta & Nadir Khayat

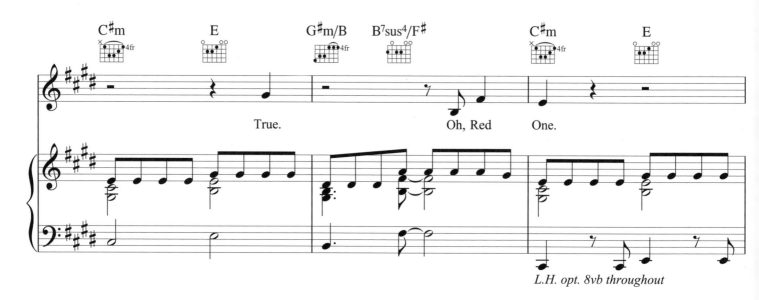

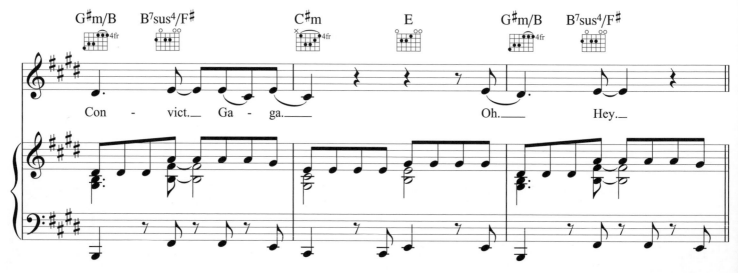

N.C.

1. I've had a lit-tle bit too much. (Much)_ All of the peo-ple start to
2. Wish I could shut my play-boy mouth. (Mouth)_ How'd I turn my shirt in-side

rush._ (Start to rush by.) A diz-zy twist-er dance, can't find my drink, oh man.
out?_ (In-side out, right.) Con-trol your poi-son, babe, ros-es have thorns, they say.

Where are my keys? I lost my phone._ (Phone)_
And we're all get-ting hosed to-night._ (Night)_

What's go - ing on on the floor?_ I love this re-cord, ba-by,

(Spoken) Let's go!

Half psy-chot-ic, sick, hyp-not - ic, got my blue-print it's sym-phon - ic. Half psy-chot-ic, sick, hyp-not-

-ic, got my blue-print e - lec-tron - ic. Half psy - chot-ic, sick, hyp-not-

-ic, got my blue-print it's sym-phon - ic. Half psy - chot - ic, sick, hyp-not-

Jar Of Hearts

Christina Perri

Words & Music by Christina Perri,
Drew Lawrence & Barrett Yeretsian

Just The Way You Are

Billy Joel

As performed by Diana Krall

Words & Music by Billy Joel

Modern Latin Ballad ♩ = 120

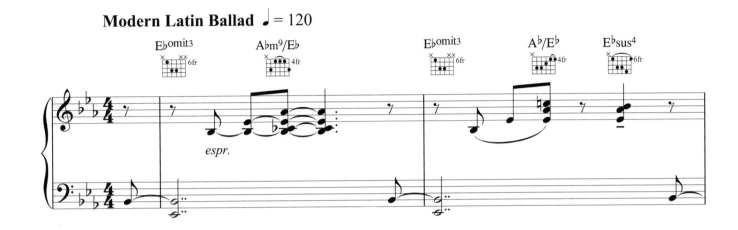

espr.

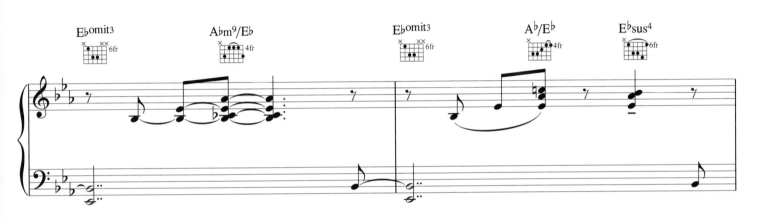

1° Rubato
2° Latin

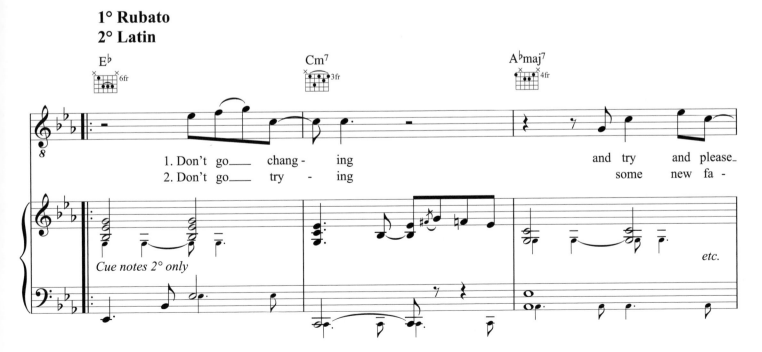

1. Don't go___ chang - ing
2. Don't go___ try - ing

and try   and please___
some   new fa -

Cue notes 2° only

etc.

190

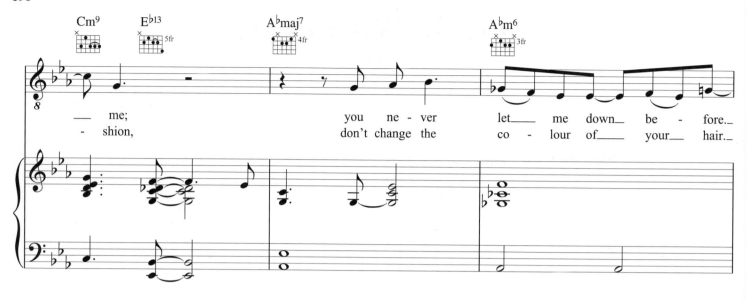

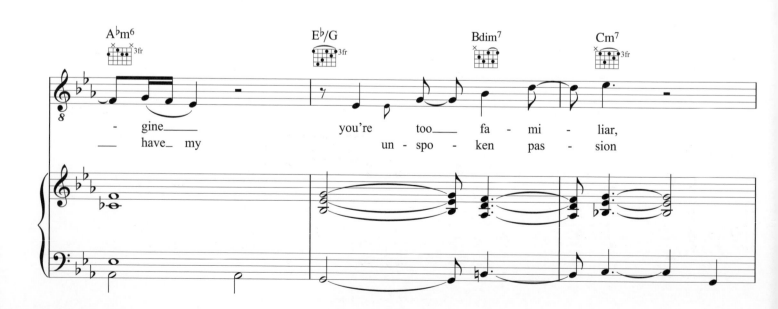

and I don't see you a - ny - more.
al - though I might not seem to care.

A tempo, latino

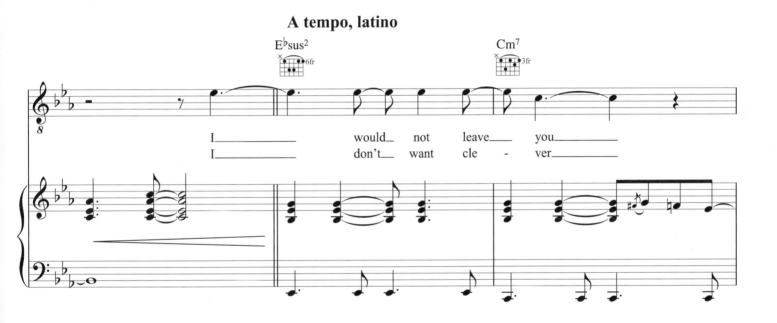

I would not leave you
I don't want cle - ver

in times of trou - ble; we ne - ver
con - ver - sa - tion, I ne - ver

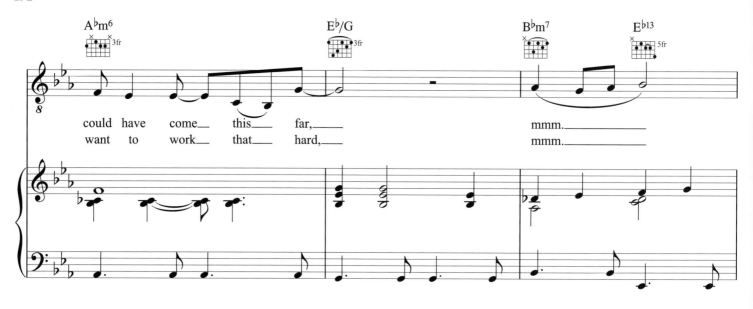

could have come__ this__ far,____ mmm._____
want to work__ that__ hard,____ mmm._____

I took____ the____ good____ times,
I just____ want____ some - one

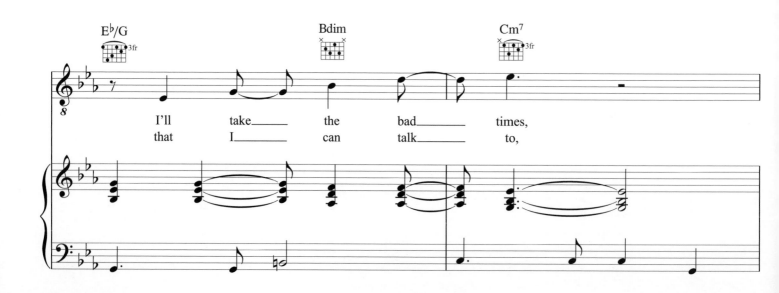

I'll take____ the bad_____ times,
that I____ can talk____ to,

I'll take you just____ the way____ you____ are.____
I want you just____ the way____ you____ are.____

I need to know___ that you___ will al - - ways___ be___

the same old some - one that___ I knew.___

___ Oh_____ what will it take___

'till you___ be - lieve_____ in___ me?___

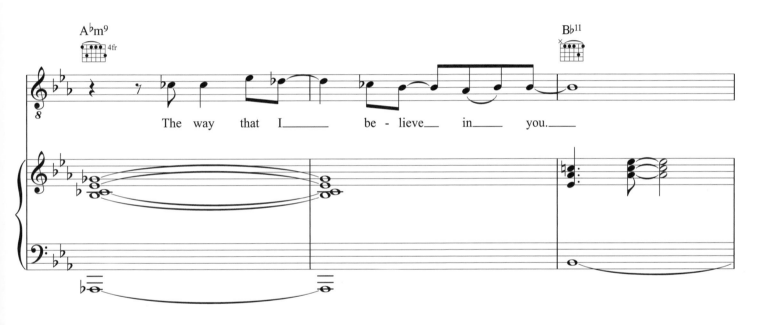

The way that I_____ be - lieve___ in____ you.___

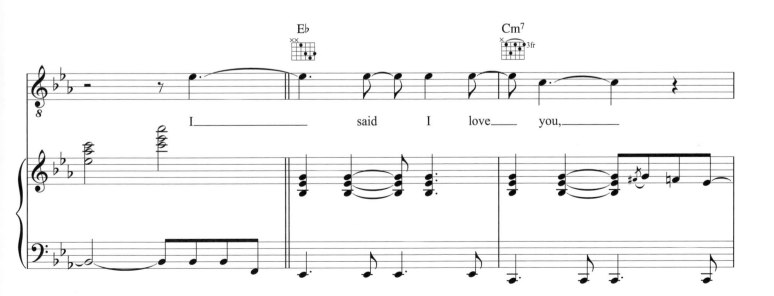

I_____ said I love___ you,_____

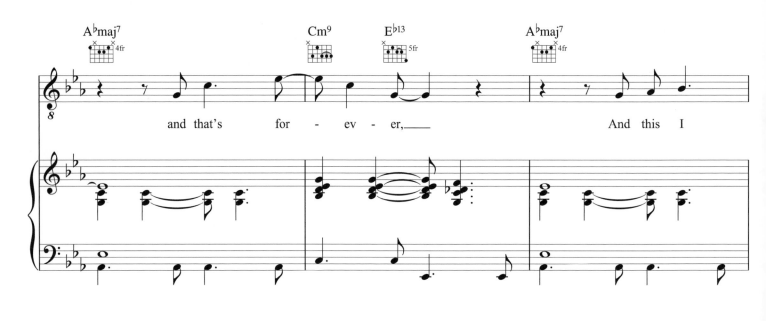

and that's for - ev - er,____ And this I

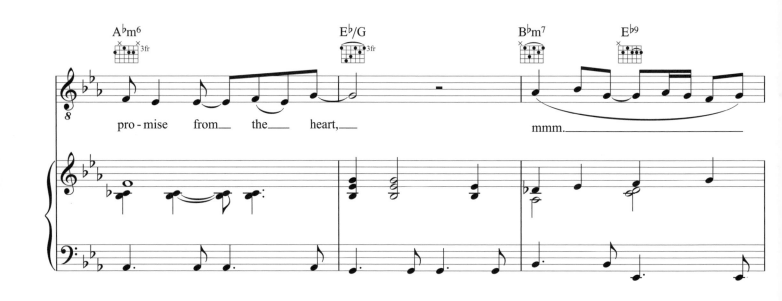

pro - mise from____ the____ heart,____ mmm._____

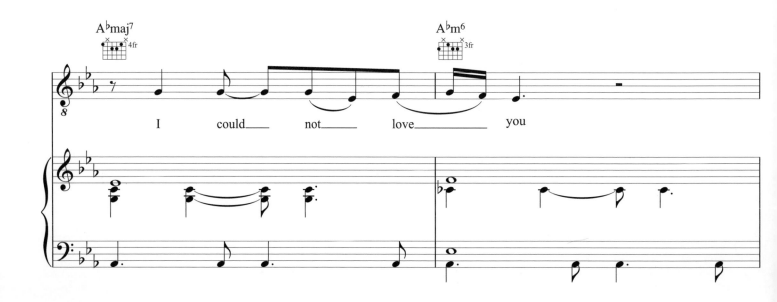

I could____ not____ love_____ you

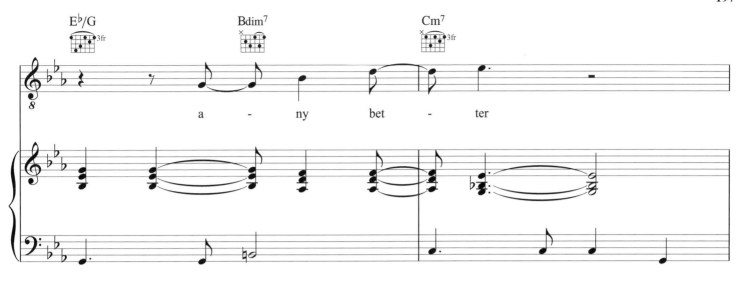

a - ny bet - ter

I love____ you just____ the way_____ you are.____

rall.

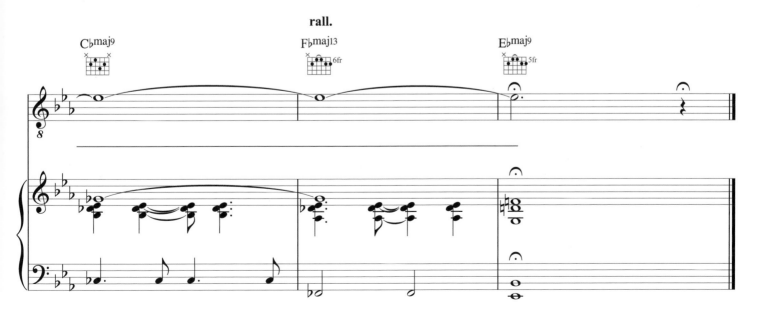

Killing Me Softly With His Song

Roberta Flack

Words by Norman Gimbel
Music by Charles Fox

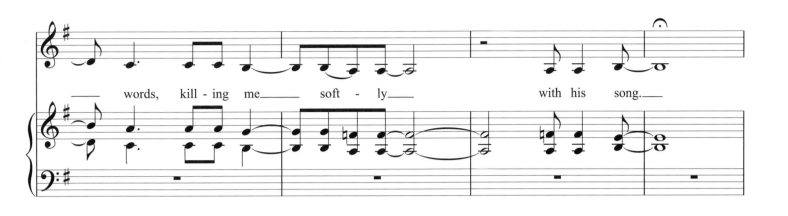

words, kill-ing me____ soft - ly____ with his song.____

N.C.

8 bars rhythm

1. I heard he sang____ a good____ song,
(Verse 2 see block lyrics)

I____ heard he had a style,____ and so I came____

____ to see____ him and listen for____ a while.____

Verse 2:
I felt all flushed with fever,
Embarrassed by the crowd,
I felt he found my letters
And read each one out loud,
I prayed that he would finish
But he just kept right on...

Lean On Me

Bill Withers

Words & Music by Bill Withers

Let It Be

The Beatles

Words & Music by John Lennon & Paul McCartney

Live While We're Young

One Direction

Words & Music by Savan Kotecha,
Carl Falk & Rami Yacoub

1. Hey, girl I'm wait-ing on you. I'm wait-ing on you.

Come on and let me sneak you out. And have a ce-le-bra-tion.

Love Story

Taylor Swift

Words & Music by Taylor Swift

Moderately

Make You Feel My Love

Adele

Words & Music by Bob Dylan

1. When the rain is blow-ing in your face, and the whole world is on
2. When the eve-ning shad-ows and the stars ap-pear, and there is no - one there to dry

228

no doubt in my mind where you be- long.___
you ain't seen noth- ing like me yet.

3. I'd go hun- gry, I'd___ go___ black and blue,___
4. I could make you hap- py, make your dreams come true,___

I'd go crawl- ing down the av - e - nue.___ Know there's noth- ing___ that I___
noth- ing that I would - n't do. Go to the ends of the

would - n't do___ to make you feel my love.___
earth for you___ to make you feel my love,___

Man In The Mirror

Michael Jackson

Words & Music by Glen Ballard & Siedah Garrett

My Cherie Amour

Stevie Wonder

Words & Music by Stevie Wonder, Henry Cosby & Sylvia Moy

Verse 2

In a café or sometimes on a crowded street,

I've been near you but you never noticed me.

My Cherie Amour, won't you tell me how could you ignore,

That behind that little smile I wore,

How I wish that you were mine.

Verse 3

Maybe someday you'll see my face among the crowd,

Maybe someday I'll share your little distant cloud.

Oh, Cherie Amour, pretty little one that I adore,

You're the only girl my heart beats for,

How I wish that you were mine.

My Heart Will Go On

Céline Dion

Words by Will Jennings
Music by James Horner

Con pedale

My Girl

The Temptations

Words & Music by William "Smokey" Robinson & Ronald White

No One

Alicia Keys

Words & Music by Alicia Keys,
George Harry & Kerry Brothers, Jr.

Rise

Gabrielle

Words & Music by Bob Dylan, Gabrielle,
Ferdy Unger-Hamilton & Ollie Dagois

Verse 2:
Caught up in my thinking, yeah
Like a prisoner in my mind.
You pose so many questions
That the truth is hard to find.
I'd better think twice, I know
That I'll get over you.

Look at my life *etc.*

Run

Snow Patrol

Words & Music by Gary Lightbody, Jonathan Quinn,
Mark McClelland, Nathan Connolly & Iain Archer

Someone Like You

Adele

Words & Music by Adele Adkins & Daniel Wilson

Smooth

Santana

Words by Rob Thomas
Music by Itaal Shur & Rob Thomas

Medium Latin Rock

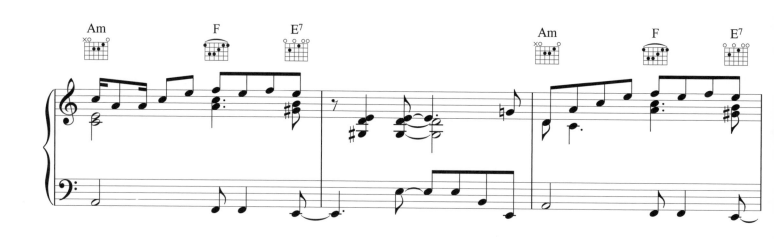

Man, it's a

be so smooth,___ Give me your heart.__ Make it real or else for-get a-bout it.

Well, I'll tell you

This Love

Maroon 5

Words & Music by Adam Levine, James Valentine,
Jesse Carmichael, Mickey Madden & Ryan Dusick

1. I was___ so high___ I did___ not re-cog-nise___ the fire___ burn-ing
2. I tried___ my best___ to feed her ap-pe-tite,___ to keep her com-ing

Take A Bow

Rihanna

Words & Music by Mikkel Eriksen,
Tor Erik Hermansen & Shaffer Smith

The Way It Is

Bruce Hornsby

Words & Music by Bruce Hornsby

That's just the way it is,___

D.S. al Coda

that's_ just the way it is.___ 3. Well they

$\oplus$ *Coda*

that's just the way it is,___ it is,___ it is,___ it

is.___

Time After Time

Cyndi Lauper

Words & Music by Cyndi Lauper & Robert Hyman

Viva La Vida

Coldplay

Words & Music by Guy Berryman, Jon Buckland,
Will Champion & Chris Martin

Thriller

Michael Jackson

Words & Music by Rod Temperton

F♯/C♯

C♯m7

1. It's close to mid - night,___ and some-thin' e-vil's lurk-in' in the dark.___
2. You hear the door___ slam___ and re - al - ize there's no-where left to run.___
3. They're out to get___ you.___ There's de - mons clos - in' in on ev-'ry - side.___

F♯/C♯

Un - der the moon - light___ you
You feel the cold___ hand,___ and
They will pos - sess___ you___ un -

I'm gon-na thrill you to -

C#m   A/C#   B/C#   F#/C#   Repeat ad lib. to fade

-night. (*See spoken lyrics*)

Spoken lyrics:
Darkness falls across the land
The midnight hour is close at hand
Creatures crawl in search of blood
To terrorize y'all's neighbourhood
And whosoever shall be found
Without the soul for getting down
Must stand and face the hounds of hell
And rot inside a corpse's shell.

The foulest stench is in the air
The funk of forty thousand years
And grizzly ghouls from every tomb
Are closing in to seal your doom
And though you fight to stay alive
Your body starts to shiver
For no mere mortal can resist
The evil of the thriller.

Walking In Memphis

Marc Cohn

Words & Music by Marc Cohn

prayer._____ But boy, you've got a prayer in Mem-

- phis. Now

Mu - ri-el plays pi - a - no ev-'ry Fri - day at the Hol - ly-wood,___ and they

brought me down___ to see her and they asked me if I would.___

We Belong Together

Mariah Carey

Words & Music by Mariah Carey, Jermaine Dupri,
Kenneth Edmonds, Manuel Seal, Bobby Womack, Darnell Bristol,
Sidney Johnson, Johnta Austin, Patrick Moten & Sandra Sully

We've Only Just Begun

The Carpenters

Words by Paul Williams
Music by Roger Nichols

What A Fool Believes

The Doobie Brothers

Words & Music by Kenny Loggins & Michael McDonald

Yesterday

The Beatles

Words & Music by John Lennon & Paul McCartney

1. Yes - ter - day___ all my trou - bles seemed so far a - way. Now it looks as though they're

You're Beautiful

James Blunt

Words & Music by Sacha Skarbek,
James Blunt & Amanda Ghost

My life is bril - liant.

Your Song

Elton John

Words & Music by Elton John & Bernie Taupin

1. It's a lit-tle bit fun-ny,_____ this feel - ing in - side._____
2. If I was a sculp-tor,_____ but then a-gain no,_____ or a
(Verses 3 & 4 see block lyrics)

I'm not one of those_ who_ can ea - si - ly hide._____
man_____ who makes pot -ions in_ the tra-vel-ling show._

Verse 3:
I sat on the roof and kicked off the moss.
Well, a few of the verses, well, they've got me quite cross,
But the sun's been quite kind while I wrote this song;
It's for the people like you that keep it turned on.

Verse 4:
So excuse me forgetting, but these things I do;
You see I've forgotten if they're green or they're blue.
Anyway, the thing is, what I really mean;
Yours are the sweetest eyes I've ever seen.

And you can tell everybody *etc.*